TEA DRINKING IN 18TH CENTURY AMERICA

Its Etiquette and Equipage

By
Rodris Roth
Jennifer C. Petersen

© Copyright 2017
By
Tea Trade Mart Publishing Co.

800 NE Tenney Road, 110-107
Vancouver, WA 98685
www.TeaTradeMart.com

All rights reserved.
No part of this book may be reproduced in any form by electronic or mechanical means without written permission from Tea Trade Mart except for a brief media review.

Printed and manufactured in
The United States of America.
ISBN-13:
978-1976220869

ISBN-10:
1976220866

ABOUT:

Jennifer Petersen

Jennifer Petersen lives alongside a creek in a quiet old-growth forest in the State of Washington. A "Southern Lady" by heritage, born in the Western North Carolina area of the Blue Ridge Mountains, her interest in history and genealogy grew because of tracing her Irish and English ancestors who arrived in Virginia around 1528. Jennifer's lineage includes ancestors from many different countries and she is Cherokee Proud.

Jennifer Petersen is a tea business development consultant and a masterful tea blender to the trade. She helps tea professionals start a tea business and she develops tea training programs for food and beverage companies.

The director of Create+Design+Manage a Profitable Tea Business, Ms. Petersen is a professional trainer who conducts online and on-site training seminars. A graduate of the Protocol School of Washington®, Petersen's programs include tea etiquette, social etiquette, and business protocol. Ms. Petersen is a member of volunteer service groups such as Specialty Tea Institute, Specialty Tea Institute's Tea Advisory Board, DAR Fort Vancouver Chapter, the Clark County Genealogical Society, and Women Entrepreneur's Organization.

TEA DRINKING IN 18TH-CENTURY AMERICA: ITS ETIQUETTE AND EQUIPAGE
Rodris Roth

An English Family at Tea. Detail from an oil painting attributed to Joseph Van Aken, about 1720. In collection of Victoria and Albert Museum. Crown Copyright. (Color plate courtesy of the *Saturday Book.*)

Tea Drinking in 18th-Century America:

Its Etiquette and Equipage—

By Rodris Roth

Annotations: Jennifer C. Petersen

In 18th-century America, the pleasant practice of taking tea at home was an established social custom with a recognized code of manners and distinctive furnishings. Pride was taken in a correct and fashionable tea table whose equipage included much more than teapot, cups, and saucers.

It was usually the duty of the mistress to make and pour the tea; and it was the duty of the guests to be adept at handling a teacup and saucer and to provide social "chitchat". Because of the expense and time involved, the tea party was limited to the upper classes; consequently, such an affair was a status symbol. The cocktail party of the 20th century has, perhaps, replaced the tea party of the 18th century as a social custom, reflecting the contrast between the relaxed atmosphere of yesterday with the hurried pace of today.

THE AUTHORS: *Miss Roth is assistant curator of cultural history in the United States National Museum, Smithsonian Institution. Ms. Petersen is a Certified Tea Specialist and Certified Etiquette and Protocol Consultant*

The Americans "use much tea", noted the Abbé Robin during his visit to this country in 1781. "The greatest mark of civility and welcome they can show you, is to invite you to drink it with them."[1]

Tea was the social beverage of the 18th century; serving it was a sign of politeness and hospitality, and drinking it was a custom with distinctive manners and specific equipment. Most discussions of the commodity have dealt only with its political, historical, or economic importance; however, in order to understand the place tea holds in this country's past, it also is important to consider the beverage in terms of the social life and traditions of the Americans. As the Abbé Robin pointed out, not only was tea an important commodity on this side of the Atlantic, but the imbibing of it was an established social practice.

An examination of teatime behavior and a consideration of what utensils were used or thought appropriate for tea drinking are of help in reconstructing and interpreting American history as well as in furnishing and re-creating interiors of the period, thus bringing into clearer focus the picture of daily life in 18th-century America. For these reasons, and because the subject has received little attention, the present study has been undertaken.

Tea had long been known and used in the Orient before it was introduced into Europe in the early part of the 17th century. At about the same time two other new beverages appeared, chocolate from the Americas and coffee from the Near East. The presence of these commodities in European markets is indicative of the vigorous exploration and active trade of that century, which also witnessed the successful settlement of colonies in North America. By about mid-17th century the new beverages were being drunk in England, and by the 1690's were being sold in New England. At first chocolate was preferred, but coffee, being somewhat cheaper, soon replaced it and in England gave rise to a number of public places of refreshment known as coffee houses. Coffee was, of course, the primary drink of these establishments, but that tea also was available is indicated by an advertisement that appeared in an English newspaper in 1658. One of the earliest advertisements for tea, it announced:

That Excellent, and by all Physicians approved, *China* Drink, called by the *Chineans*, *Tcha*, by other nations *Tay alias Tee*, is sold at the *Sultaness-head*, a *Cophee-house* in *Sweetings* Rents by The Royal Exchange, London.[2]

For a time, tea was esteemed mainly for its curative powers, which explains why it was "by all Physicians approved". According to an English broadside published in 1660, the numerous contemporary ailments which tea "helpeth" included "the headaches, giddiness, and heaviness". It was also considered "good for colds, dropsies and scurvies and [it] expelleth infection. It prevents and cures agues, surfeits and fevers."[3] By the end of the 17th century, however, tea's medicinal qualities had become secondary to its fashionableness as a unique drink. Tea along with the other exotic and novel imports from the Orient such as fragile porcelains, lustrous silks, and painted wallpapers had captured the European imagination. Though the beverage was served in public pleasure gardens as well as coffee houses during the early 1700's in England, social tea drinking in the home was gradually coming into favor. The coffee houses continued as centers of political, social, and literary influence as well as of commercial life into the first half of the 19th century, for apparently Englishmen preferred to drink their coffee in public rather than private houses and among male rather than mixed company. This was in contrast to tea, which was drunk in the home with breakfast or as a morning beverage and socially at afternoon gatherings of both sexes, as we see in the painting *An English Family at Tea*. As tea drinking in the home became fashionable, both host and hostess took pride in a well-appointed tea table, for a teapot of silver or fragile blue-and-white Oriental porcelain with matching cups and saucers and other equipage added prestige as well as elegance to the teatime ritual.

Figure 1. —*Family Group*, by Gawen Hamilton, about 1730. In collection of Colonial Williamsburg, Inc. The tea set, undoubtedly of porcelain, includes cups and saucers, a cream or milk container, and a sugar container with tongs. (*Photo courtesy of Colonial Williamsburg, Inc.*)

At first the scarcity and expense of the tea, the costly paraphernalia used to serve it, and the leisure considered necessary to consume it, limited the use of this commodity to the upper classes. For these reasons, social tea drinking was, understandably, a prestige custom. One becomes increasingly aware of this when looking at English paintings and prints of the early 18th century, such as *Family Group* painted by Gawen Hamilton about 1730. Family members are portrayed in the familiar setting of their own parlor with its paneled walls and comfortable furnishings. Their pet, a small dog, surveys the scene from a resting place on a corner of the carpet. Teatime appears to have just begun, for cups are still being passed around and others on the table await filling from the nearby porcelain teapot. It seems reasonable to assume, since the painting is portraiture, that the family is engaged in an activity which, although familiar, is considered suitable to the group's social position and worthy of being recorded in oil. That tea drinking was a status symbol also is indicated by the fact that the artist has used the tea ceremony as the theme of the picture and the tea table as the focal point.

Eighteenth-century pictures and writings are basic source materials for information about Anglo-American tea drinking. A number of the pictures are small-scale group or conversation piece paintings of English origin in which family and friends are assembled at tea, similar to *Family Group*, and they provide pictorial information on teatime modes and manners. The surroundings in which the partakers of tea are depicted also reveal information about the period and about the gracious living enjoyed in the better homes. Paneled walls and comfortable chairs, handsome chests and decorative curtains, objects of ceramic and silver and glass, all were set down on canvas or paper with painstaking care, and sometimes with a certain amount of artistic license. A careful study of these paintings provides an excellent guide for furnishing and reconstructing period rooms and exhibits, even to the small details such as objects on mantels, tables, and chests, thus further documenting data from newspapers, journals, publications, and writings of the same period.

In America, as in England, tea had a rather limited use as a social beverage during the early 1700's. Judge Samuel Sewall, the recorder-extraordinary of Boston life at the turn of the 17th century, seems to have mentioned tea only once in his copious diary. In the entry for April 15, 1709, Sewall wrote that he had attended a meeting at the residence of Madam Winthrop where the guests "drunk Ale, Tea, Wine."[4] At this time ale and wine, in contrast to tea, were fairly common drinks. Since tea and the equipment used to serve it were costly, social tea drinking was restricted to the prosperous and governing classes who could afford the luxury. The portrayal of the rotund silver teapot and other tea-drinking equipment in such an American painting as *Susanna Truax* done by an unknown painter in 1730, indicates that in this country as in England not only was the tea ceremony of social importance but also that a certain amount of prestige was associated with the equipage. And, the very fact that an artist was commissioned for a portrait of this young girl is suggestive of a more than ordinary social status of the sitter and activity depicted.

Figure 2. *Susanna Truax*, an American painting dated 1730. In collection of Edgar William and Bernice Chrysler Garbisch, National Gallery of Art. On the beige, marble-like table top beside Susanna—who wears a dress of red, black, and white stripes—are a fashionable silver teapot and white ceramic cup, saucer, and sugar dish. (*Photo courtesy National Gallery of Art.*)

English customs were generally imitated in this country, particularly in the urban centers. Of Boston, where he visited in 1740, Joseph Bennett observed that "the ladies here visit, drink tea and indulge every little piece of gentility to the height of the mode and neglect the affairs of their families with as good grace as the finest ladies in London."[5] English modes and manners remained a part of the social behavior after the colonies became an independent nation. Visitors to the newly formed United States were apt to remark about such habits as tea drinking, as did Brissot de Warville in 1788, that "in this, as in their whole manner of living, the Americans in general resemble the English."[6] Therefore, it is not surprising to find that during the 18th century the serving of tea privately in the morning and socially in the afternoon or early evening was an established custom in many households.

The naturalist Peter Kalm, during his visit to North America in the mid-18th century, noted that tea was a breakfast beverage in both Pennsylvania and New York. From the predominantly Dutch town of Albany in 1749 he wrote that "their breakfast is tea, commonly without milk". At another time, Kalm[7] stated:

With the tea was eaten bread and butter or buttered bread toasted over the coals so that the butter penetrated the whole slice of bread. In the afternoon about three o'clock tea was drunk again in the same fashion, except that bread and butter was not served with it.

This tea-drinking schedule was followed throughout the colonies. In Boston the people "take a great deal of tea in the morning," have dinner at two o'clock, and "about five o'clock they take more tea, some wine, madeira [and] punch,"[8] reported the Baron Cromot du Bourg during his visit in 1781. The Marquis de Chastellux confirms his countryman's statement about teatime, mentioning that the Americans take "tea and punch in the afternoon."[9]

During the first half of the 18th century the limited amount of tea available at prohibitively high prices restricted its use to a proportionately small segment of the total population of the colonies. About mid-century, however, tea was beginning to be drunk by more and more people, as supplies increased and costs decreased, due in part to the propaganda and merchandising efforts of the East India Company. According to Peter Kalm, tea, chocolate, and coffee had been "wholly unknown" to the Swedish population of Pennsylvania and the surrounding area before the English arrived, but in 1748 these beverages "at present constitute even the country people's daily breakfast."[10] A similar observation was made a few years later by Israel Acrelius:[11]

Tea, coffee, and chocolate are so general as to be found in the most remote cabins, if not for daily use, yet for visitors, mixed with Muscovado, or raw sugar.

America was becoming a country of tea drinkers. Then, in 1767, the Townshend Act imposed a duty on tea, among other imported commodities. Merchants and citizens in opposition to the act urged a boycott of the taxed articles. A Virginia woman, in a letter[12] to friends in England, wrote in 1769:

> ... I have given up the Article of Tea, but some are not quite so tractable; however, if we can convince the good folks on your side the Water of their Error, we may hope to see happier times.

In spite of the tax many colonists continued to indulge in tea drinking. By 1773 the general public, according to one Philadelphia merchant, "can afford to come at this piece of luxury" while one-third of the population "at a moderate computation, drink tea twice a day."[13] It was at this time, however, that efforts were made to enforce the English tea tax and the result was that most famous of tea parties, the "Boston Tea Party."

Thereafter, an increasing number of colonists abstained from tea drinking as a patriotic gesture. Philip Fithian, a tutor at Nomini Hall, the Virginia plantation of Col. Robert Carter, wrote in his journal on Sunday, May 29, 1774:

> After dinner, we had a Grand & agreeable Walk in & through the Gardens—There is great plenty of Strawberries, some Cherries, Goose berries &c.—Drank Coffee at four, they are now too patriotic to use tea.

And indeed they were patriotic, for by September the taste of tea almost had been forgotten at Nomini Hall, as Fithian vividly recounted in his journal:[14]

Something in our palace this Evening, very merry happened—Mrs. *Carter* made a dish of Tea. At Coffee, she sent me a dish—& the Colonel both ignorant—He smelt, sipt—look'd—At last with great gravity he asks what's this? —Do you ask Sir—Poh! —And out he throws it splash a sacrifice to Vulcan.

Figure 3. —*A Society of Patriotic Ladies* at Edenton in North Carolina pledging to drink no more tea, 1775, an engraving published by R. Sayer and J. Bennet, London. In Print and Photograph Division, Library of Congress. (*Photo courtesy of Library of Congress.*)

Other colonists, in their own way, also showed their distaste for tea (see fig. 3). Shortly before the outbreak of the American Revolution there appeared in several newspapers an expression of renouncement in rhyme, "A Lady's Adieu to Her Tea-Table"[15] (below), which provides a picture of contemporary teatime etiquette and equipage.

A Lady's Adieu to Her Tea-Table

FAREWELL the Tea-board with your gaudy attire,
Ye cups and ye saucers that I did admire;
To my cream pot and tongs, I now bid adieu;
That pleasure's all fled that I once found in you.
Farewell pretty chest that so lately did shine,
With hyson and congou and best double fine;
Many a sweet moment by you I have sat,
Hearing girls and old maids to tattle and chat;
And the spruce coxcomb laughs at nothing at all,
Only some silly work that might happen to fall.
No more shall my teapot so generous be
In filling the cups with this pernicious tea,
For I'll fill it with water and drink out the same,
Before I'll lose LIBERTY that dearest name,
Because I am taught (and believe it is fact)
That our ruin is aimed at in the late act,
Of imposing a duty on all foreign Teas,
Which detestable stuff we can quit when we please.
LIBERTY'S The Goddess that I do adore,
And I'll maintain her right until my last hour,
Before she shall part I will die in the cause,
For I'll never be govern'd by tyranny's laws.

Many people gave up tea for the duration of the war and offered various substitute beverages such as coffee and dried raspberry leaves, "a detestable drink" which the Americans "had the heroism to find good," remarked a postwar visitor, Léon Chotteau.[16] Although the colonists had banished tea "with enthusiasm," the tea habit was not forgotten. Chotteau further noted that "they all drink tea in America as they drink wine in the South of France". Tea drinking continued to be an important social custom in the new nation well into the 19th century.

The tea ceremony, sometimes simple, sometimes elaborate, was the very core of family life. Moreau de St. Méry observed in 1795, during his residence in Philadelphia, that "the whole family is united at tea, to which friends, acquaintances and even strangers are invited."[17] That teatime hospitality was offered to the newest of acquaintances or "even strangers" is verified by Claude Blanchard. He wrote of his visit to Newport, Rhode Island, on July 12, 1780, that "in the evening there was an illumination. I entered the house of an inhabitant, who received me very well; I took tea there, which was served by a young lady". And while staying in Boston, Blanchard mentioned that a new acquaintance "invited us to come in the evening to take tea at his house. We went there; the tea was served by his daughter."[18]

In the daily routine of activities when the hour for tea arrived, Moreau de St. Méry remarked that "the mistress of the house serves it and passes it around."[19] In the words of another late-18th-century diarist, the Marquis de Barbé-Marbois, those present might "seat themselves at a spotless mahogany table, and the eldest daughter of the household or one of the youngest married women makes the tea and gives a cup to each person in the company." *Family Group* (fig. 1) provides an illustration of this practice in the early part of the century. During the tea hour social and economic affairs were discussed, gossip exchanged, and, according to Barbé-Marbois, "when there is no news at all, they repeat old stories."[20] Many entries in Nancy Shippen's journal[21] between 1783 and 1786 indicate that this Philadelphian passed many such hours in a similar manner. On March 11, 1785, she wrote: "About 4 in the Afternoon, D. Cutting came in, & we spent the afternoon in the most agreeable chit-chat manner, drank a very good dish of Tea together & then separated". Part of an undated entry in December 1783 reads: "This Afternoon we were honor'd with the Company of Gen'l Washington to Tea, Mrs. & Major Moore, Mrs. Stewart, Mr. Powell, Mr. B Washington, & two or 3 more". If acquaintances of Nancy's own age were present or the company large, the tea hour often extended well into the evening with singing, conversing, dancing, and playing of whist, chess, or cards. Of one such occasion she wrote:[21]

> Mrs. Allen & the Miss Chews drank Tea with me & spent the even'g. There was half a dozen agreeable & sensible men that was of the party. The conversation was carried on in the most sprightly, agreeable manner, the Ladies bearing by far the greatest part—till nine when cards was proposed, & about ten, refreshments were introduced which concluded the Evening.

Obviously, young men and women enjoyed the sociability of teatime, for it provided an ideal occasion to get acquainted. When the Marquis de Chastellux was in Philadelphia during the 1780's he went one afternoon to "take tea with Madam Shippen", and found musical entertainment to meet with his approval and a relationship between the sexes which had parental sanction. One young miss played on the clavichord, and "Miss Shippen sang with timidity but a very pretty voice", accompanied for a time by Monsieur Otto on the harp. Dancing followed, noted the Marquis, "while mothers and other grave personages conversed in another room."[22] In New York as in Philadelphia teatime was an important part of the younger set's social schedule. Eliza Bowne, writing to her sister in January 1810, reported that "as to news—New York is not so gay as last Winter, few balls but a great many tea-parties."[23] The feminine interest and participation in such gatherings of personable young men and attractive young women was expressed by Nancy Shippen[24] when she wrote in her journal after such a party:

"Saturday night at 11 o'clock. I had a very large company at Tea this Evening. The company is but just broke up, I don't know when I spent a more merry Even'g. We had music, Cards, &c &c."

A masculine view of American tea parties was openly voiced by one foreign visitor, Prince de Broglie, who, upon arrival in America in 1782, "only knew a few words of English, but knew better how to drink excellent tea with even better cream, how to tell a lady she was pretty, and a gentleman he was sensible, by reason whereof I possessed all the elements of social success."[25] Similar feelings were expressed by the Comte de Ségur during his sojourn in America in the late 18th century when, in a letter to his wife in France, he wrote: "My health continues excellent, despite the quantity of tea one must drink with the ladies out of gallantry, and of madeira all day long with the men out of politeness."[26]

Festive tea parties such as the ones described above are the subject of some of the group portraits or conversation pieces painted about 1730 by the English artist William Hogarth. *The Assembly at*

Wanstead House, now in the Philadelphia Museum of Art, illustrates quite an elegant affair taking place in a large, richly decorated, English interior. The artist has filled the canvas with people standing and conversing while a seated group plays cards at a table in the center of the room. To one side near the fireplace a man and two women drinking tea are seated at an ornately carved, square tea table with a matching stand for the hot water kettle. On a dish or circular stand in the center of the table is a squat teapot with matching cups and saucers arranged in parallel rows on either side.

Tea-drinking guests seem to have been free to sit or stand according to their own pleasure or the number of chairs available, and Barbé-Marbois noted that at American tea parties "people change seats, some go, others come". The written and visual materials offer little in the way of evidence to suggest that in general men stood and women sat during teatime. In fact, places at the tea table were taken by both sexes, even at formal tea parties such as the one depicted in *The Assembly at Wanstead House*.

A less formal but more usual tea scene is the subject of another Hogarth painting, *The Wollaston Family*, now in the Leicester Art Gallery, England. The afternoon gathering has divided into two groups, one playing cards, the other drinking tea. An atmosphere of ease and comfort surrounds the party. The men and women seated at the card table are discussing the hand just played, while the women seated about the square tea table in front of the fireplace are engaged in conversation. A man listens as he stands and stirs his tea. Each drinker holds a saucer with a cup filled from the teapot on a square tile or stand in the center of the table. One woman is returning her cup, turned upside down on the saucer, to the table. More about this particular habit later.

The same pleasant social atmosphere seen in English paintings seems to have surrounded teatime in America, as the previously cited entries in Nancy Shippen's journal book suggest. Her entry for January 18, 1784,[27] supplies a description that almost matches *The Wollaston Family*:

"A stormy day, alone till the afternoon; & then was honor'd with the Company of Mr. Jones (a gentleman lately from Europe) Mr. Du Ponceau, & Mr. Hollingsworth at Tea—We convers'd on a variety of subjects & play'd at whist, upon the whole spent an agreeable Even'g".

Tea was not only a beverage of courtship; it also was associated with marriage. Both Peter Kalm, in 1750, and Moreau de St. Méry, in the 1790's, report the Philadelphia custom of expressing good wishes to a newly married couple by paying them a personal visit soon after the marriage. It was the duty of the bride to serve wine and punch to the callers before noon and tea and wine in the afternoon.[28]

No doubt, make-believe teatime and pretend tea drinking were a part of some children's playtime activities. Perhaps many a little girl played at serving tea and dreamed of having a tea party of her own, but few were as fortunate as young Peggy Livingston who, at about the age of five, was allowed to invite "by card ... 20 young misses" to her own "Tea Party & Ball". She "treated them with all good things, & a violin", wrote her grandfather. There were "5 coaches at ye door at 10 when they departed. I was much amused 2 hours."[29]

Figure 4. —*Conversazioni*, by W. H. Bunbury, published 1782. In Print and Photograph Division, Library of Congress.

Tea seems to have been the excuse for many a social gathering, large or small, formal, or informal. And sometimes an invitation to drink tea meant a rather elegant party. "That is to say," wrote one cosmopolitan observer of the American scene in the 1780's, the Marquis de Chastellux, "to attend a sort of assembly pretty much like the *conversazioni* [social gathering] of Italy; for tea here, is the substitute for the *rinfresco* [refreshment]."[30] A view of such an event has been depicted in the English print *Conversazioni* (fig. 4), published in 1782. It is hoped that the stiffly seated and solemn-faced guests

became more talkative when the tea arrived.

However, this tea party may have been like the ones Ferdinand Bayard attended in Bath, Virginia, of which he wrote: "The only thing you hear, while they are taking tea, is the whistling sound made by the lips on edges of the cups. This music is varied by the request made to you to have another cup."[31] At tea parties, cakes, cold pastries, sweetmeats, preserved fruits, and plates of cracked nuts might also be served, according to Mrs. Anne Grant's reminiscences of pre-Revolutionary America.[32] Peter Kalm noted during his New York sojourn in 1749 that "when you paid a visit to any home" a bowl of cracked nuts and one of apples were "set before you, which you ate after drinking tea and even at times while partaking of tea."[33] Sometimes wine and punch were served at teatime, and "in summer," observed Barbé-Marbois, "they add fruit and other things to drink."[34] Coffee too might be served. As the Frenchman Claude Blanchard explained:[35]

They [the Americans] do not take coffee immediately after dinner, but it is served three or four hours afterwards with tea; this coffee is weak and four or five cups are not equal to one of ours; so that they take many of them. The tea, on the contrary, is very strong. This use of tea and coffee is universal in America.

Dealing with both food and drink at the same time was something of an art. It was also an inconvenience for the uninitiated, and on one occasion Ferdinand Bayard, a late-18th-century observer of American tea ritual, witnessed another guest who, "after having taken a cup [of tea] in one hand and tartlets in the other, opened his mouth and told the servant to fill it for him with smoked venison!"[36]

While foreign visitors recognized that the "greatest mark of courtesy" a host and hostess could offer a guest was a cup of tea, hospitality could be "hot water torture" for foreigners unless they understood the social niceties not only of holding a cup and tartlet, but of declining without offending by turning the cup upside down and placing a spoon upon it. The ceremony of the teaspoon is fully explained by the Prince de Broglie who, during his visit to Philadelphia in 1782, reported the following teatime incident at the home of Robert Morris:[37]

I partook of most excellent tea and I should be even now still drinking it, I believe, if the [French] Ambassador had not charitably notified me at the twelfth cup, that I must put my spoon across it when I wished to finish with this sort of warm water. He said to me: it is almost as ill-bred to refuse a cup of tea when it is offered to you, as it would [be] indiscreet for the mistress of the house to propose a fresh one, when the ceremony of the spoon has notified her that we no longer wish to partake of it.

Bayard reports that one quick-witted foreigner, uninformed as to the teaspoon signal, had had his cup filled again and again until he finally "decided after emptying it to put it into his pocket until the replenishments had been concluded."[38]

Figure 5. —*Tea Party in the Time of George I*, an English painting of about 1725. In collection of Colonial Williamsburg, Inc. The silver equipage includes (left to right) a sugar container and cover, hexagonal tea canister, hot water jug or milk jug, slop bowl, teapot, and (in front) sugar tongs, spoon boat or tray, and spoons. The cups and saucers are Chinese export porcelain. (*Photo courtesy of Colonial Williamsburg, Inc.*)

The gracious art of brewing and serving tea was as much an instrument of sociability as was a bit of music or conversation. This custom received the attention of a number of artists, and it is amazing what careful and detailed treatment they gave to the accessories of tea. We are familiar with the journals, newspaper advertisements, and other writings that provide contemporary reports on this custom, but it is to the artist we turn for a more clearly defined view. The painter saw, arranged, and gave us a visual image—sometimes richly informative, as in *Tea Party in the Time of George I* (fig. 5)—of the different tea time items and how they were used. The unknown artist of this painting, done about 1725, has carefully illustrated each piece of equipment considered appropriate for the tea ceremony and used for brewing the tea in the cups held with such grace by the gentleman and child.

Throughout the 18th century the well-equipped tea table would have displayed most of the items seen in this painting: a teapot, slop bowl, container for milk or cream, tea canister, sugar container, tongs, teaspoons, and cups and saucers. These pieces were basic to the tea ceremony and, with the addition of a tea urn which came into use during the latter part of the 18th century, have remained the established tea equipage up to the present day. Even a brief investigation of about 20 inventories—itemized lists of the goods and property of deceased persons that were required by law—reveal that in New York between 1742 and 1768 teapots, cups and saucers, teaspoons, and tea canisters were owned by both low and high-income groups in both urban and rural areas.

The design and ornament of the tea vessels and utensils, of course, differed according to the fashion of the time, and the various items associated with the beverage provide a good index of the stylistic changes in the 18th century. The simple designs and unadorned surfaces of the plump pear-shaped teapot in *Tea Party in the Time of George I* (fig. 5) and the spherical one seen in the portrait *Susanna Truax* (fig. 2) mark these pieces as examples of the late baroque style popular in the early part of the 18th century. About mid-century, teapots of inverted pear-shape, associated with the rococo style, began to appear. A pot of this shape is depicted in the portrait *Paul Revere* painted about 1765 by John Singleton Copley and owned by the Museum of Fine Arts, Boston. The fact that a teapot was chosen as an example of Revere's craft, from all of the objects he made, indicates that such a vessel was valued as highly by its maker as by its owner. The teapot was a mark of prestige for both craftsman and hostess. Apparently, the famous silversmith and patriot was still working on the piece, for the nearby tools suggest that the teapot was to have engraved and chased decoration, perhaps of flowers, scrolls, and other motifs typical of the rococo style. The restrained decoration and linear outlines of the teapot illustrated in the print titled *The Old Maid* (fig. 14) and the straight sides and oval shape of the teapot belonging to a late 18th-century child's set (fig. 6) of Chinese export porcelain are characteristics of the neoclassic style that was fashionable at the end of the century. Tea drinkers were extremely conscious of fashion changes and, whenever possible, set their tea tables with stylish equipment in the prevailing fashion. Newspaper advertisements, journals, letters, and other written materials indicate that utensils in the "best and newest taste" were available, desired, purchased, and used in this country.

Figure 6. —Part of a child's tea set of Chinese export porcelain, or "painted China", made about 1790. The painted decoration is of pink roses and rose buds with green leaves; the border is orange, with blue flowers. At one time, this set probably included containers for cream or milk and sugar, as did the adult "tea table setts complete". (*USNM 391761; Smithsonian photo 45141-B.*)

Further verification of the types and kinds of equipage used is supplied by archeological investigations of colonial sites. For instance, sherds or fragments of objects dug from or near the site of a dwelling at Marlborough, Virginia, owned and occupied by John Mercer between 1726 and 1768, included a silver teaspoon made about 1735 and two teapot tops—one a pewter lid and the other a Staffordshire salt-glaze cover made about 1745—as well as numerous pieces of blue-and-white Oriental porcelain cups and saucers (fig. 7). Such archeological data provides concrete proof about tea furnishings used in this country. A comparison of sherds from colonial sites with wares used by the English and of English origin indicates that similar types of equipage were to be found upon tea tables in both countries. This also substantiates the already cited American practice of following English modes and manners, a practice Brissot de Warville noted in 1788 when he wrote that in this country "tea forms, as in England, the basis of the principal parties of pleasures."[39]

Figure 7. —Fragments of teacups of Chinese export porcelain with blue decoration on white, excavated at the site of John Mercer's dwelling at Marlborough, Virginia, 1726-1768. These sherds, now in the United States National Museum, are from cups similar in shape and decoration to the ones depicted in figures 1 and 5. (*USNM 59.1890, 59.1969, 59.1786; Smithsonian photo 45141-G.*)

Tea furnishings, when in use, were to be seen upon rectangular tables with four legs, square-top and circle-top tripods, and Pembroke tables. Such tables were, of course, used for other purposes, but a sampling of 18th-century Boston inventories reveals that in some households all or part of the tea paraphernalia was prominently displayed on the tea table rather than being stored in cupboards or closets. A "Japan'd tea Table & China" and "a Mahogany Do. &

China", both in the "Great Room", are listed in Mrs. Hannah Pemberton's inventory recorded in Boston in 1758. The inventory of Joseph Blake of Boston recorded in 1746 lists a "tea Table with a Sett of China furniture" in the back room of the house, while in the "closett" in the front room were "6 Tea Cups & Saucers" along with other ceramic wares.[40]

The most popular type of tea table apparently was the circular tripod; that is, a circular top supported on a pillar with three feet. This kind of table is seen again and again in the prints and paintings (figs. 1, 2, 9, 14), and is listed in the inventories of the period. These tables, usually of walnut or mahogany, had stationary or tilt tops with plain, scalloped, or carved edges. Square or round, tripod or four-legged, the tables were usually placed against the wall of the room until teatime when, in the words of Ferdinand Bayard, "a mahogany table is brought forward and placed in front of the lady who pours the tea."[41] This practice is depicted in a number of 18th-century pictures, with the tea table well out in the room, often in front of a fireplace, and with seated and standing figures at or near the table (fig. 1). Evidence of such furniture placement in American parlors is recorded in a sketch and note Nancy Shippen received from one of her beaus, who wrote in part:[42]

... this evening I passed before Your house and seeing Company in the parlour I peep'd through the Window and saw a considerable Tea Company, of which by their situation I could only distinguish four persons. You will see the plan of this Company upon the next page.

Figure 8. —A sketch by Louis Guillaume Otto that was enclosed in a letter to Nancy Shippen of Philadelphia about 1780. The sketch indicates the placement of the furniture in the Shippen parlor and the location of the tea-party participants. The "Explication" accompanying the drawing reads in part: "*A.* Old Dr. Shippen sitting before the Chimney.... *B.* Mr. Lee walking up and down, speaking and laughing by intervalls.... *C.* Miss Nancy [Shippen] before the tea table.... *D.* Mrs. Shippen lost in sweet meditations. *E. F. G.* Some strangers which the Spy [Mr. Otto] could not distinguish. *H.* Cyrus [the butler] standing in the middle of the room—half asleep. *I.* Mr. Otto standing before the window...". From Shippen Papers, Manuscripts Division, Library of Congress.

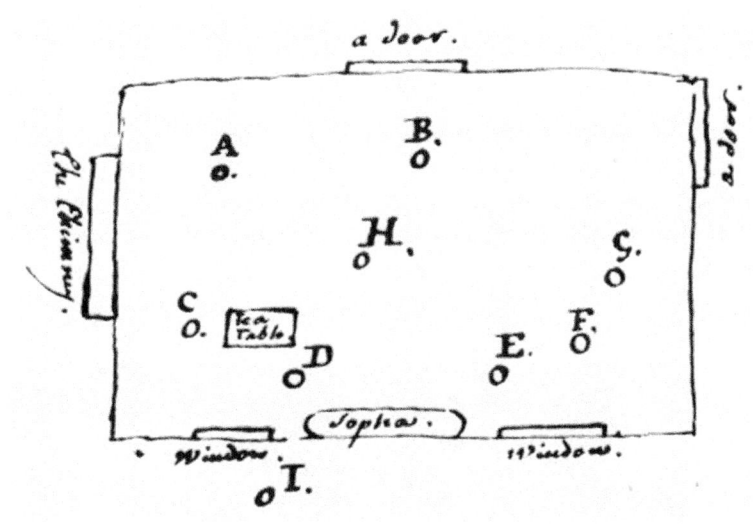

In the sketch (fig. 8), a floor plan of the Shippen parlor, we can see the sofa against the wall between the windows, while chairs and tea table have been moved out in the room. The table is near the fireplace, where Miss Shippen served the tea. In the 18th century, such an arrangement was first and foremost one of comfort, and perhaps also one of taste. The diary of Jacob Hiltzheimer indicates that in 1786 the first signs of fall were felt on August 1, for the Philadelphian wrote: "This evening it was so cool that we drank tea by the fire."[43] In the south as in the north, tea—or, at the time of the American Revolution its patriotic substitute, coffee—was served by the fire as soon as the first winter winds were felt. Philip Fithian, while at Nomini Hall in Virginia, wrote in his journal on September 19, 1774: "the Air is clear, cold & healthful. We drank our Coffee at the great House very sociably, round a fine Fire, the House and Air feels like winter again."[44]

Figure 9. —*The Honeymoon*, by John Collett, about 1760. In the midst of a domestic scene replete with homey details, the artist has depicted with care the tea table and its furnishing, including a fashionable tea urn symbolically topped with a pair of affectionate birds. (*Photo courtesy of Frick Art Reference Library.*)

Table cloths—usually square white ones (as in fig. 9) that showed folds from having been stored in a linen press—were used when tea was served, but it is difficult to say with any certainty if their use depended upon the whim of the hostess, the type of table, or the time of day. A cloth probably was used more often on a table with a plain top than on one with scalloped or carved edges. However, as can be seen in *Family Group* (fig. 1) and *An English Family at Tea* (frontispiece), it was perfectly acceptable to serve tea on a plain-top table without a cloth. Apparently such tables were also used at breakfast or morning tea, because Benjamin Franklin, in a letter from London dated February 19, 1758, gave the following directions for the use of "six coarse diaper Breakfast Cloths" which he sent to his wife: "they are to spread on the Tea Table, for nobody breakfasts here on the naked Table, but on the Cloth set a large Tea Board with the Cups."[45] Some of the 18th-century paintings depicting tea tables with cloths do deal with the morning hours, as indicated by their titles or internal evidence, as in *The Honeymoon* (fig. 9) painted by John Collett about 1760. In this scene of domestic confusion and bliss, a tray or teaboard has been placed on the cloth, illustrating Franklin's comment about English breakfast habits. Cloths may also be seen in pictures in which the time of day cannot be determined. Therefore, the use of a cloth at teatime may in truth have depended upon the hostess's whim if not her pocketbook.

In addition, trays or teaboards of various sizes and shapes were sometimes used. They were usually circular or rectangular in form, occasionally of shaped or scalloped outline. Some trays were supported upon low feet; others had pierced or fretwork galleries or edges to prevent the utensils from slipping off. Wood or metal was the usual material, although ceramic trays were also used. At large gatherings a tray was often employed for passing refreshments (fig. 4). "A servant brings in on a silver tray the cups, the sugar bowl, the cream jugs, pats of butter, and smoked meat, which are offered to each individual," explained Ferdinand Bayard.[46] The principal use of the tray was, of course, to bring the tea equipage to the table. Whether placed on a bare or covered table, it arrived with the various pieces such as cups and saucers, spoons, containers for sugar and cream or milk, tongs, bowls, and dishes arranged about the teapot.

Figure 10. —Pieces of a tea set of Crown-Derby porcelain, dating about 1790. The cups and saucers, covered sugar bowl, container for cream or milk, plate and bowls are ornamented with gilt borders and a scattering of blue flowers on a white ground (*USNM 54089-54095; Smithsonian photo 45541-A.*)

Such tea furnishings of ceramic were sold in sets; that is, all pieces being of the same pattern. Newspaper advertisements in the 1730's specifically mention "Tea Setts," and later in the century ceramic imports continue to include "beautiful compleat Tea-Setts" (fig. 10). In the early 18th century, tea sets of silver were uncommon if not actually unique, though pieces were occasionally made to match existing items, and, in this way, a so-called set similar to the pieces seen in *Tea Party in the Time of George I* (fig. 5) could be formed. However, by the latter part of the century the wealthier hostesses were able to purchase from among a "most elegant assortment of Silver Plate ... compleat Tea and Coffee services, plain and rich engraved."[47] When of metal, tea sets (fig. 11) usually consisted of a teapot, containers for sugar and cream or milk, and possibly a slop bowl, while ceramic sets, such as the one seen in *Family Group* (fig. 1), included cups and saucers as well.

Figure 11. —Silver tea set consisting of teapot, sugar bowl, container for cream or milk, and waste bowl, made by John McMullin, of Philadelphia, about 1800. Matching coffee and hot water pot made by Samuel Williamson, also of Philadelphia. The letter "G", in fashionable script, is engraved on each piece. (*USNM 37809; Smithsonian photo 45541.*)

While the tea set illustrated in *Family Group* appears to have all the basic pieces, it can hardly be considered a "complete" tea set when compared with the following porcelain sets listed in the 1747 inventory of James Pemberton of Boston:

One sett Burnt China Containing 12 Cups& Saucers Slop Bowl Tea Pot Milk Pot boat for spoons, tea Cannister Sugar Dish 5 Handle Cups plate for the Tea Pot & a white Tea Pot   Value [£]20

One set Blue & white do. contg. 12 Cups & saucers Slop Bowl 2 plates Sugr. Dish Tea Pot 6 Handle Cups & white tea Pot   Value [£]10

In addition, the Pemberton inventory lists a silver tea pot and "1 pr. Tea Tongs & Strainer," items that were undoubtedly used with the ceramic sets.[48]

Tea sets were even available for the youngest hostess, and the "several compleat Tea-table Sets of Children's cream-colored [ceramic] Toys" mentioned in a Boston advertisement of 1771 no doubt added a note of luxury to make-believe tea parties during playtime.[49] The pieces in children's tea sets, such as the ones pictured from a child's set of Chinese export porcelain (fig. 6), usually were like those of regular sets and differed only in size. Little Miss Livingston must have been happy, indeed, when her uncle wrote[50] that he had sent

... a compleat tea-apparatus for her Baby [doll]. Her Doll may now invite her Cousins Doll to tea, & parade her tea table in form. This must be no small gratification to her. It would be fortunate if happiness were always attainable with equal ease.

The pieces of tea equipage could be purchased individually. For instance, teacups and saucers, which are differentiated in advertisements from both coffee and chocolate cups, regularly appear in lists of ceramic wares offered for sale, such as "very handsome Setts of blue and white China Tea-Cups and Saucers," or "enamell'd, pencill'd and gilt (fig. 12), red and white, blue and white, enamell'd and scallop'd (fig. 13), teacups and saucers."[51] These adjectives used by 18th-century salesmen usually referred to the types and the colors of the decorations that were painted on the pieces. "Enameled" most likely meant that the decorations were painted over the glaze, and "penciled" may have implied motifs painted with a fine black line of pencil-like appearance, while "gilt", "red and white", and "blue and white" were the colors and types of the decoration. Blue and white china was, perhaps, the most popular type of teaware, for it regularly appears in newspaper advertisements and inventories and among sherds from colonial sites (fig. 7).

Figure 12.—Cup and saucer of Chinese export porcelain with scalloped edges and fluting. The painted decoration of black floral design on the side of the cup is touched with gold; the borders are of intersecting black vines and ribbons. (*USNM 284499; Smithsonian photo 45141-D.*)

Figure 13. —Hand-painted Staffordshire creamware teacup excavated at the site of a probable 18th-century and early 19th-century china shop in Newburyport, Massachusetts. Decoration consists of a brown band above a vine border with green leaves and blue berries over orange bellflowers. The spiral fluting on the body and the slight scalloping on the edge of this cup are almost identical with that on the cup held by Mrs. Calmes in figure 15. (*USNM 397177-B; Smithsonian photo 45141-C.*)

Concerning tea, the Abbé Robin went so far as to say that "there is not a single person to be found, who does not drink it out of china cups and saucers."[52] However exaggerated the statement may be, it does reflect the popularity and availability of Chinese export porcelain in the post-Revolutionary period when Americans were at last free to engage in direct trade with the Orient. Porcelain for the American market was made in a wide variety of forms, as well as in complete dinner and tea sets, and was often decorated to special order. Hand painted monograms, insignia of various kinds, and patriotic motifs were especially popular. A tea set decorated in this way was sent to Dr. David Townsend of Boston, a member of the Society of the Cincinnati, by a fellow member of the Society, Maj. Samuel Shaw, American consul at Canton. In a letter to Townsend from Canton, China, dated December 20, 1790, Shaw wrote:

Accept, my dear friend, as a mark of my esteem and affection, a tea set of porcelain, ornamented with the Cincinnati and your cypher. I hope shortly after its arrival to be with you, and in company with your amiable partner, see whether a little good tea improves or loses any part of its flavor in passing from one hemisphere to the other.

Appended to the letter was the following inventory,[53] which provides us with a list of the pieces deemed essential for a fashionably set tea table:

2 tea pots & stands

Sugar bowl & do

Milk ewer

Bowl & dish

6 breakfast cups & saucers

12 afternoon do

Porcelain, however, had long been a part of China-trade cargos to Europe and from there to America. The early shipments of tea had included such appropriate vessels for the storage, brewing, and drinking of the herb as tea jars, teapots, and teacups. The latter were small porcelain bowls without handles, a form which the Europeans and Americans adopted and continued to use throughout the 18th century for tea, in contrast to the deeper and somewhat narrower cups, usually with handles, in which chocolate and coffee were served. Even after Europeans learned to manufacture porcelain early in the 18th century, the ware continued to be imported from China in large quantities and was called by English-speaking people, "china" from its country of origin. Porcelain also was referred to as "India china ware", after the English and continental East India Companies, the original traders and importers of the ware. "Burnt china" was another term used in the 18th century to differentiate porcelain from pottery.

Whatever the ware, the teacups and saucers, whether on a tray, the cloth, or a bare table, were usually arranged in an orderly manner about the teapot, generally in rows on a rectangular table or tray and in a circle on a round table or tray. In the English conversation piece painting titled *Mr. and Mrs. Hill in Their Drawing Room,* by Arthur Devis about 1750, the circular tripod tea table between the couple and in front of the fireplace is set in such a way. The handleless teacups on saucers are neatly arranged in a large semicircle around the rotund teapot in the center that is flanked on one side by a bowl and on the other by a jug for milk or cream and a sugar container. Generally, cups and saucers were not piled one upon the other but spread out on the table or tray where they were filled with tea and then passed to each guest.

Figure 14. —*The Old Maid*, an English cartoon published in 1777. In Print and Photograph Division, Library of Congress. Although the Englishwoman apparently is defying established tea etiquette by drinking from a saucer and allowing the cat on the table, her tea furnishings appear to be in proper order. The teapot is on a dish and the teakettle is on its own special stand, a smaller version of the tripod tea table.

The Old Maid
The lady here you see display'd,
By some is styled an ancient maid
But if her inward thoughts you'd view,
She thinks herself as young as you.
Oh! Puss forbear to lick the cream,
Your mistress longs to do the same.

Pictures show male and female guests holding both cup and saucer or just the cup. An English satirical print, *The Old Maid* (fig. 14), published in 1777, was the only illustration found that depicted an individual using a dish for tea, or, to be exact, a saucer. In the 18th century, a dish of tea was in reality a cup of tea, for the word "dish" meant a cup or vessel used for drinking as well as a utensil to hold food at meals. A play on this word is evident in the following exchange reported by Philip Fithian between himself and Mrs. Carter, the mistress of Nomini Hall, one October forenoon in 1773: "Shall I help you, Mr. Fithian, to a Dish of Coffee?—I choose a deep Plate, if you please Ma'am, & Milk."[54] The above suggests that the practice of saucer sipping, while it may have been common among the general public, was frowned upon by polite society. The fact that Americans preferred and were "accustomed to eat everything hot" further explains why tea generally was drunk from the cup instead of the saucer. According to Peter Kalm, "when the English women [that is, of English descent] drank tea, they never poured it out of the cup into the saucer to cool it, but drank it as hot as it came from the teapot."[55] Later in the century another naturalist, C. F. Volney, also noted that "very hot tea" was "beloved by Americans of English descent."[56] From this it would appear that "dish of tea" was an expression rather than a way of drinking tea in the 18th century. On the table, a saucer seems always to have been placed under the cup whether the cup was right side up or upside down.

Figure 15. —*Mrs. Calmes*, by G. Frymeier, 1806. In Calmes-Wright-Johnson Collection, Chicago Historical Society. The cup and saucer (or bowl), possibly hand-decorated Staffordshire ware or Chinese export porcelain, are decorated with dark blue bands and dots, wavy brown band, and a pink rose with green foliage. (*Photo courtesy of Chicago Historical Society.*)

Teaspoons, when in use, might be placed on the saucer or left in the cups. The portrait titled *Mrs. Calmes* (fig. 15), painted by G. Frymeier in 1806, indicates that handling a cup with the spoon in it could be accomplished with a certain amount of grace. Teaspoons also were placed in a pile on the table or in a silver "Boat for Tea Spoons," or more often in such ceramic containers as "Delph Ware ... Spoon Trays," or blue-and-white or penciled china "spoon boats."[57]

Figure 16. —Silver tongs in the rococo style, made by Jacob Hurd, of Boston, about 1750. (*USNM 383530; Smithsonian photo 45141.*)

Tongs were especially suited for lifting the lumps of sugar from their container to the teacup. During the 18th century both arched and scissor type tongs were used. Instead of points, the latter had dainty flat grips for holding a lump of sugar (fig. 16). The early arched tongs were round in section, as are the pair illustrated in *Tea Party in the Time of George I* (fig. 5), while tongs made by arching or bending double a flat strip of silver (fig. 17) date from the second half of the 18th century. These articles of tea equipage, variously known as "tongs," "tea tongs," "spring tea tongs," and "sugar tongs," were usually made of silver, though "ivory and wooden tea-tongs" were advertised in 1763.[58] According to the prints and paintings of the period, tongs were placed in or near the sugar container. Teaspoons were also used for sugar, as illustrated in the painting *Susanna Truax* (fig. 2). Perhaps young Miss Truax is about to indulge in a custom favored by the Dutch population of Albany as reported by Peter Kalm in 1749: "They never put sugar into the cup, but take a small bit of it into their mouths while they drink."[59]

Figure 17. —Silver tongs made by William G. Forbes, of New York, about 1790. In the United States National Museum. The engraved decoration of intersecting lines is typical of the neoclassic style. A variant of this motif appears as the painted border on a porcelain cup and saucer of the same period (fig. 12). (*USNM 59.474; Smithsonian photo 45141-A.*)

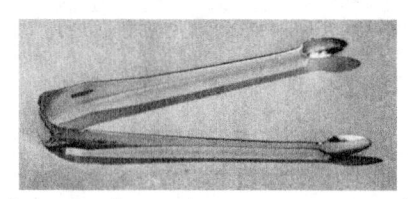

Shallow dishes, such as the one seen in the portrait *Susanna Truax*, and hemispherical bowls were used as containers for sugar. Often called "sugar dishes" or just "sugars," they were available in delftware, glass (fig. 18), and silver as well as in blue-and-white, burnt, enameled, and penciled china. Some containers were sold with covers, and it has been suggested that the saucer-shaped cover of the hemispherical sugar dish or bowl, fashionable in the first half of the 18th century, also served as a spoon tray. However, in the painting *Tea Party in the Time of George I* (fig. 5) the cover is leaning against the bowl and the spoons are in an oval spoon tray or boat. Another possibility, if the lid was multipurpose, is that it was used as a dish or stand under the teapot to protect the table top. Silver sugar boxes, basins, and plated sugar baskets were other forms used to hold sugar,[60] which, in whatever container, was a commodity important to the Americans. As Moreau de St. Méry noted, they "use great quantities in their tea."[61]

Figure 18. —Stiegel-type, cobalt-blue glass sugar dish with cover, made about 1770. (*USNM 38922; Smithsonian photo 42133-D.*)

Containers for cream or milk may be seen in many of the 18th-century teatime pictures and are found in the advertisements of the period under a variety of names. There were cream pots of glass and pewter and silver (figs. 19 and 20), jugs of penciled and burnt china, and in the 1770's one could obtain "enameled and plain three footed cream jugs" from Mr. Henry William Stiegel's glass factory at Manheim, Pennsylvania. There were cream pails, urns, and ewers of silver plate, and plated cream basins "gilt inside."[62] Milk pots, used on some tea tables instead of cream containers, were available in silver, pewter, ceramic, and "sprig'd, cut and moulded" glass.[63] Although contemporary diarists and observers of American customs seem not to have noticed whether cream was served cold and milk hot, or if tea drinkers were given a choice between cream and milk, the Prince de Broglie's comment already cited concerning his ability to drink "excellent tea with even better cream" and the predominance of cream over milk containers in 18th-century advertisements would seem to indicate that in this country cream rather than milk was served with tea in the afternoon.

Figure 19. —Silver creamer made by Myer Myers, of New York, about 1750. The fanciful curves of the handle and feet are related to the rococo design of the sugar tongs in figure 16. (*USNM 383553; Smithsonian photo 45141-F.*)

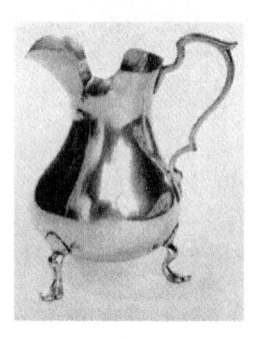

Figure 20. —Silver creamer made by Simeon A. Bayley, of New York, about 1790. The only ornamentation is the engraving of the initials "R M" below the pouring lip. (*USNM 383465; Smithsonian photo 45141-E.*)

Silver creamer made by John McMullin 1790-1850/

While the Americans, as the Europeans, added cream or milk and sugar to their tea, the use of lemon with the beverage is questionable. Nowhere is there any indication that the citrus fruit was served or used with tea in 18th-century America. Punch seems to have been the drink with which lemons were associated.

Often a medium-sized bowl, usually hemispherical in shape, is to be seen on the tea table, and it is most likely a slop bowl or basin. According to advertisements these bowls and basins were available in silver, pewter, and ceramic.[64] Before a teacup was replenished, the remaining tea and dregs were emptied into the slop bowl. Then the cup might be rinsed with hot water and the rinsing water discarded in the bowl. The slop basin may also have been the receptacle for the mote or foreign particles—then inherent in tea but now extracted by mechanical means—that had to be skimmed off the beverage in the cup. In England, this was probably done with a small utensil known to present day collectors as a mote spoon or mote skimmer. Although the exact purpose of these spoons remains unsettled, it seems likely that they were used with tea. It has been suggested that the perforated bowl of the spoon was used for skimming foreign particles off the tea in the cup and the tapering spike-end stem to clear the clogged-up strainer of the teapot spout. The almost complete absence of American-made mote spoons suggests that these particular utensils were seldom used here.

Possibly the "skimmer" advertised in 1727 with other silver tea pieces was such a spoon.[65] No doubt, tea strainers (fig. 21) were also used to insure clear tea. The tea dregs might then be discarded in the slop bowl or left in the strainer and the strainer rested on the bowl. However, only a few contemporary American advertisements and inventories have been found which mention tea strainers.[66] Punch strainers, though generally larger in size, seem to have doubled as tea strainers in some households. The 1757 inventory of Charles Brockwell of Boston includes a punch strainer which is listed not with the wine glasses and other pieces associated with punch but with the tea items: "1 Small Do. [china] Milk Pot 1 Tea Pot 6 Cups & 3 Saucers & 1 Punch Strainer."[67] Presumably, the strainer had last been used for tea.

Figure 21. —Silver strainer made by James Butler, of Boston, about 1750. The handle's pierced pattern of delicate, curled vines distinguishes this otherwise plain strainer. (*USNM 383485; Smithsonian photo 44828-J.*)

The teapot was, of course, the very center of the social custom of drinking tea; so, it usually was found in the center of the tray or table. At first, only teapots of Oriental origin imported with the cargos of tea were available, for the teapot had been unknown to Europeans before the introduction of the beverage. However, as tea gained acceptance as a social drink and the demand for equipage increased, local craftsmen were stimulated to produce wares that could compete with the Chinese imports. Teapots based on Chinese models and often decorated with Chinese motifs were fashioned in ceramic and silver. No doubt many an 18th-century hostess desired a silver teapot to grace her table and add an elegant air to the tea ceremony. A lottery offering one must have raised many a hope, especially if, as an advertisement of 1727 announced, the "highest Prize consists of an Eight Square Tea-Pot", as well as "six Tea-Spoons, Skimmer and Tongs". By the end of the century "an elegant silver tea-pot with an ornamental lid, resembling a Pine-apple" would have been the wish of a fashion-conscious hostess. Less expensive than silver, but just as stylish according to the merchants' advertisements were "newest fashion teapots" of pewter or, in the late 18th century, Britannia metal teapots. The latest mode in ceramic ware also was to be found upon the tea table. In the mid-18th century it was "English brown China Tea-Pots of Sorts, with a rais'd Flower" (probably the ceramic with a deep, rich brown glaze known today as Jackfield-type ware), "black", "green and Tortois" (a pottery glazed with varigated colors in imitation of tortoise shell), and "Enameled Stone" teapots. At the time of the American Revolution, teaware imports included "Egyptian, Etruscan, embossed red China, agate, green, black, colliflower, white, and blue and white stone enamelled, striped, fluted, pierced and plain Queen's ware tea pots."[68] (Note: Paul Revere with silver teapot.)

Sometimes the teapot, whether ceramic, pewter, or silver, was placed upon a dish or small, tile-like stand with feet. These teapot stands served as insulation by protecting the surface of the table or tray from the damaging heat of the teapot. Stands often were included in tea sets but also were sold individually, such as the "Pencil'd China ... tea pot stands," advertised in 1775, and the "teapot stands" of "best London plated ware" imported in 1797.[69] The stands must have been especially useful when silver equipage was set on a bare table top; many of the silver teapots of elliptical shape with a flat base, so popular in the latter part of the 18th century, had matching stands raised on short legs to protect the table from the expanse of hot metal. On occasion, the teapot was placed on a spirit lamp or burner to keep the beverage warm.

In most instances, it was the hot water kettle that sat upon a spirit lamp or burner rather than a teapot. Kettles were usually related to the form of contemporary teapots, but differed in having a swing handle on top and a large, rather flat base that could be placed over the flame. Advertisements mention teakettles of copper, pewter, brass, and silver, some "with lamps and stands."[70] The actual making of tea was part of the ceremony and was usually done by the hostess at the tea table. This necessitated a ready supply of boiling water close at hand to properly infuse the tea and, as Ferdinand Bayard reported, it also "weakens the tea or serves to clean up the cups."[71] Thus, the kettle and burner on their own individual table or stand were placed within easy reach of the tea table. According to 18th-century pictures the kettle was an important part of the tea setting, but it seldom appeared on the tea table. Special stands for kettles generally were made in the same form as the tea tables, though smaller in scale (fig. 14). The square stands often had a slide on which to place the teapot when the hot water was poured into it.

Both pictures and advertisements reveal that by the 1770's the tea urn was a new form appearing at teatime in place of the hot water kettle. Contrary to its name, the tea urn seldom held tea. These large silver or silver-plated vessels, some of which looked like vases with domed covers, usually had two handles on the shoulders and a spout with a tap in the front near the bottom. "Ponty pool, japanned, crimson, and gold-striped Roman tea urns" imported from Europe were among the fashionable teawares advertised at the end of the 18th century.[72] The urn might be placed on a stand of its own near the table or on the tray or table in the midst of the other equipage as it is in the painting titled *The Honeymoon* (fig. 9). Wherever placed, it signified the newest mode in teatime furnishings. One Baltimorean, O. H. Williams, in a letter dated April 12, 1786, to a close friend, enthusiastically explained that "Tea& Coffee Urns plated (mine are but partially plated and are extremely neat) are the genteelest things of the sort used now at any House & tables inferior to the first fortunes."[73]

Figure 22. —The sign of "The Tea Canister and Two Sugar Loaves" used by a New York grocer and confectioner in the 1770's. Other "tea" motifs for shop signs in the 18th century included "The Teapot", used by a Philadelphia goldsmith in 1757, and "The Tea Kettle and Stand", which marked the shop of a Charleston jeweller in 1766.

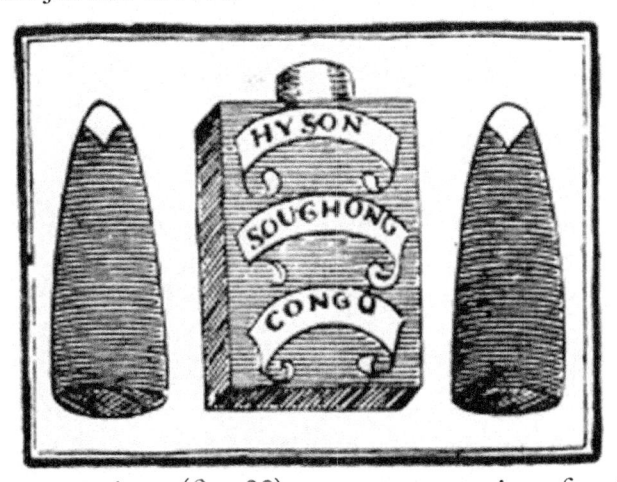

The tea canister (fig. 22), a storage container for the dry tea leaves, was yet another piece of equipment to be found on the table or tray. Ceramic canisters of blue and white, and red and gold, could be purchased to match other tea furnishings of the same ware, and silver tea canisters often were fashioned to harmonize with the silver teapots of the period. Individual canisters were produced, as well as canisters in sets of two or three. A set of canisters usually was kept in the box in which it came, a case known as a tea chest or tea caddy, such as the "elegant assortment of Tea-caddies, with one, two and three canisters" advertised in 1796.[74] Canister tops if dome-shaped were used to measure out the tea and transfer it to the teapot. Otherwise, small, short-handled spoons with broad, shallow bowls known as caddy spoons and caddy ladles were used. However, handled, the tea could have been any one of the numerous kinds available in the 18th century. Although Hyson, Souchong, and Congo, the names inscribed on the canister in [figure 22](), may have been favored, there were many other types of tea, as the following advertisement from the *Boston News-Letter* of September 16, 1736, indicates:[75]

To be Sold ... at the Three Sugar Loaves, and Cannister ... very choice Teas, viz: Bohea Tea from 22 s. to 28 s. per Pound, Congou Tea, 34 s. Pekoe Tea, 50 s. per Pound, Green Tea from 20 s. to 30 s. per Pound, fine Imperial Tea from 40 s. to 60 s. per Pound.

In the 18th century tea drinking was an established social custom with a recognized etiquette and distinctive equipage as we know from the pictures and writings of the period. At teatime men and women gathered to pursue leisurely conversations and enjoy the sociability of the home.

A study of *An English Family at Tea* ([frontispiece]()) will summarize the etiquette and equipage of the ritual—

On the floor near the table is a caddy with the top open, showing one canister of a pair. The mistress of the house, seated at the tea table, is measuring out dry tea leaves from the other canister into its lid. Members of the family stand or sit about the square tea table while they observe this first step in the ceremony. A maidservant stands ready with the hot water kettle to pour the boiling water over the leaves once they are in the teapot. In the background is the tripod kettle stand with a lamp, where the kettle will be placed until needed to rinse the cups or dilute the tea.

Not seen in this detail of the painting is the entry of a male servant who is carrying a tall silver pot, which may have contained chocolate or coffee. These two other social beverages of the 18th century were served in cups of a deep cylindrical shape, like the three seen on the end of the table. The shallow, bowl-shaped, handleless teacups and the saucers are arranged in a neat row along one side of the table. The teapot rests on a square tile-like stand or dish that protects the table from the heat. Nearby is a bowl to receive tea dregs, a pot for cream or milk, and a sugar bowl.

The teatime ritual has begun.

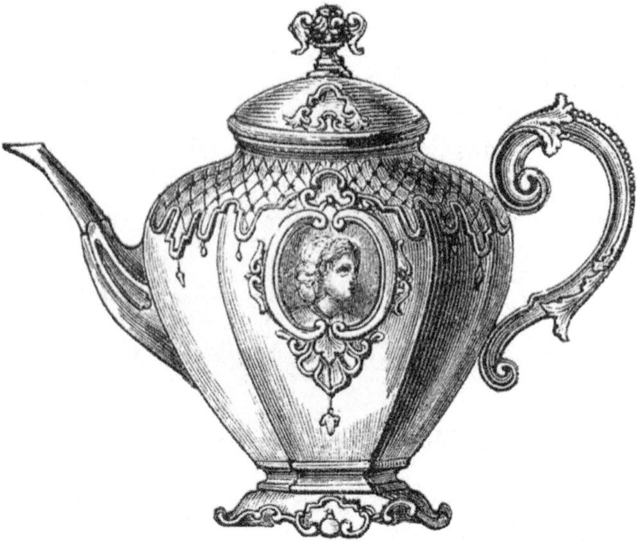

CHRONOLOGICAL LIST OF PICTURES CONSULTED

1700 ca.

Portrait Group of Gentlemen and a Child. Believed to be English or Dutch. Reproduced in Ralph Edwards, *Early Conversation Pictures from the Middle Ages to about 1730*, London, 1954, p. 117, no. 73.

1710 ca.

The Tea-Table. English. Reproduced in *The Connoisseur Period Guides: The Stuart Period, 1603-1714*, edited by Ralph Edwards and L. G. G. Ramsey, New York, 1957, p. 30.

1720 ca.

A Family Taking Tea. English. Reproduced in Edwards, *Early Conversation Pictures*, p. 132, no. 95

Two Ladies and a Gentleman at Tea. Attributed to Nicolaas Verkolje, Dutch. Reproduced in Edwards, *Early Conversation Pictures*, p. 96, no. 42.

An English Family at Tea (frontispiece). Joseph Van Aken(?). Reproduced in Percy Macquoid and Ralph Edwards, *The Dictionary of English Furniture*, revised and enlarged by Ralph Edwards, London, 1954, vol. 1, p. 10, fig. 16.

An Elegant Family Tea Gawen Hamilton - An Elegant Family Taking Tea, Hamilton, Gavin (1723-98) / Private Collection / Photo © Gavin Graham Gallery, London, UK / Bridgeman Images

1725 ca.

Tea Party in the Time of George I (fig. 5). English. Reproduced in *Antiques*, November 1955, vol. 68, p. vi following p. 460.

1730 ca.

The Assembly at Wanstead House. By William Hogarth, English. Reproduced in Edwards, *Early Conversation Pictures,* p. 125, no. 87.

Family. By William Hogarth, English. Reproduced in R. H. Wilenski, *English Painting,* London, 1933, pl. 11a.

1730 ca.

A Tea Party By William Hogarth.

Family Group (fig. 1). By Gawen Hamilton, English. Reproduced in *Antiques*, March 1953, vol. 63, p. 270.

1730

A Family Party. By William Hogarth, English. Reproduced in *English Conversation Pictures of the Eighteenth and Early Nineteenth Century*, edited by G. C. Williamson, London, 1931, pl. 10.

Susanna Truax (fig. 2). American. Reproduced in *Art in America*, May 1954, vol. 42, p. 101.

The Wollaston Family. By William Hogarth, English. Reproduced in Edwards, *Early Conversation Pictures*, p. 126, no. 88.

1731

Painting on lobed, square delft tea tray. Dutch. Reproduced in C. H. De Jorge, *Oud-Nederlandsche Majolica en Delftsch Aardewerk*, Amsterdam, 1947, p. 241, fig. 209.

1732

A Tea Party at the Countess of Portland's. By Charles Philips, English. Reproduced in Edwards, *Early Conversation Pictures*, p. 132, no. 94.

Thomas Wentworth, Earl of Strafford, with His Family. By Gawen Hamilton, English. Reproduced in Edwards, *Early Conversation Pictures*, p. 130, no. 92.

1735 ca.

The Western Family. By William Hogarth, English. Reproduced in Sacheverell Sitwell, *Conversation Pieces*, New York, 1937, no. 14.

1736 ca.

The Strode Family. By William Hogarth, English. Reproduced in Oliver Brackett, *English Furniture Illustrated*, New York, 1950, p. 168, pl. 140.

1740 ca.

The Carter Family. By Joseph Highmore, English. Reproduced in *Connoisseur*, Christmas 1934, vol. 94, p. xlv (advertisement).

1743

Painting on lobed, circular Bristol delft tea tray. English. Reproduced in F. H. Garner, *English Delftware*, New York, 1948, pl. 54.

1744 ca.

Burkat Shudi and His Family. English. Reproduced in Philip James, *Early Keyboard Instruments from Their Beginnings to the Year 1820*, New York, 1930, pl. 48.

1744

Shortly after Marriage, from *Marriage a la Mode* series. By William Hogarth, English. Reproduced in *Masterpieces of English Painting*, Chicago, 1946, pl. 3.

1745 ca.

The Gascoigne Family. By Francis Hayman, English. Reproduced in *Apollo*, October 1957, vol. 66, p. vii (advertisement).

1750 ca.

Mr. and Mrs. Hill in Their Drawing Room. By Arthur Devis, English. Reproduced in *The Antique Collector*, June 1957, vol. 28, p. 100.

1760 ca.

The Honeymoon (fig. 9). By John Collett, English. Photograph courtesy of Frick Art Reference Library, New York.

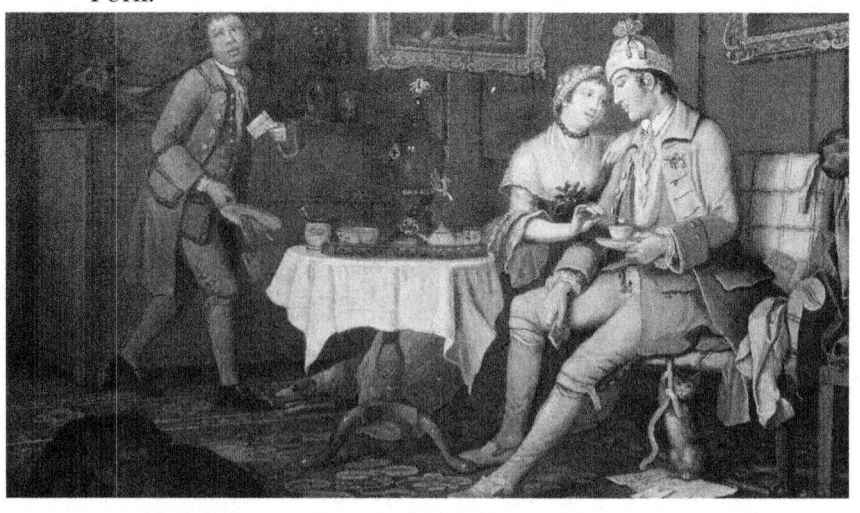

1765 ca.

Paul Revere. By John Singleton Copley, American. Reproduced in John Marshall Phillips, *American Silver*, New York, 1949, frontispiece.

1770 ca.

Lord Willoughby and Family. By John Zoffany, English. Reproduced in Lady Victoria Manners and Dr. G. C. Williamson, *John Zoffany, R. A.*, London, 1920, plate preceding p. 153.

Mr. and Mrs. Garrick at Tea. By John Zoffany, English. Reproduced in Manners and Williamson, *John Zoffany, R. A.*, plate facing p. 142.

Sir John Hopkins and Family. By John Zoffany, English. Reproduced in Manners and Williamson, *John Zoffany, R. A.*, second plate following p. 18.

The Squire's Tea. By Benjamin Wilson, English. Reproduced in *Antiques*, October 1951, vol. 60, p. 310.

1775

A Society of Patriotic Ladies (fig. 3). Engraving published by R. Sayer and J. Bennet, London. Print and Photograph Division, Library of Congress.

1777

The Old Maid (fig. 14). English. Print and Photograph Division, Library of Congress.

1780 ca.

>*The Tea Party.* By William Hamilton, English. Reproduced in *Art in America*, May 1954, vol. 42, p. 91 (advertisement).

1782

>*Conversazioni* (fig. 4). By W. H. Bunbury, English. Print and Photograph Division, Library of Congress.

1785 ca.

>*The Auriol Family* [*in India*]. By John Zoffany, English. Reproduced in Manners and Williamson, *John Zoffany, R. A.*, plate facing p. 110.

1786

>*Dr. Johnson Takes Tea at Boswell's House.* By Thomas Rowlandson, English. Reproduced in Charles Cooper, *The English Table in History and Literature*, London, 1929, plate facing p. 150.

1790 ca.

Black or the Departure for School. Engraved by J. Jones after Bigg, English. Reproduced in *Antiques*, September 1953, vol. 64, p. 163 (advertisement).

1792

Tea at the Pantheon. By Edward Edwards, English. Reproduced in William Harrison Ukers, *The Romance of Tea*, New York, 1936, plate facing p. 214.

1806

Mrs. Calmes (fig. 15). By G. Frymeier, American. Reproduced in *Antiques*, November 1950, vol. 58, p. 392.

FOOTNOTES

1. Claude C. Robin, *New Travels through North America: in a Series of Letters ... in the Year 1781*, Boston, 1784, p. 23.

2. *Mercurius Politicus*, September 23-30, 1658.

3. Edward Wenham, "Tea and Tea Things in England", *Antiques*, October 1948, vol. 54, p. 264.

4. Samuel Sewall, *Diary of Samuel Sewall, 1674-1729*, reprinted in *Collections of the Massachusetts Historical Society*, 1879, ser. 5, vol. 6, p. 253.

5. John Marshall Phillips, *American Silver*, New York, 1949, p. 76.

6. Jacques Pierre Brissot de Warville, *New Travels in the United States of America Performed in 1788*, London, 1794, p. 80.

7. Peter Kalm, *The America of 1750. Peter Kalm's Travels in North America*, edited and translated by Adolph B. Benson, New York, 1937, vol. 1, p. 346, vol. 2, p. 605.

8. Baron Cromot du Bourg, "Journal de mon Séjour en Amérique", *Magazine of American History* (1880-1881), quoted in Charles H. Sherrill, *French Memories of Eighteenth-Century America*, New York, 1915, p. 155.

9. Marquis de Chastellux, *Voyages de M. le Marquis de Chastellux dans l'Amérique Septentrionale*, Paris, 1788, quoted in Sherrill, *op. cit.* (footnote 8), p. 190.

10. Kalm, *op. cit.* (footnote 7), vol. 1, p. 195.

11. Israel Acrelius, *A History of New Sweden; or, The Settlements on the River Delaware*, translated and edited by William M. Reynolds, Philadelphia, 1874, p. 158.

12. Letter from M. Jacquelin, York, Virginia, to John Norton, London, August 14, 1769. In, *John Norton and Sons, Merchants of London and Virginia, Being the Papers from Their Counting House for the Years 1750 to 1795*, edited by Frances Norton Mason, Richmond, 1937, p. 103.

13. Letter from Gilbert Barkly to directors of the East India Company, May 26, 1773. *Tea Leaves: Being a Collection of Letters and Documents ...*, edited by Francis S. Drake, Boston, 1884, p. 200.

14. Philip Vickers Fithian, *Journal and Letters of Philip Vickers Fithian, 1773-1774; a Plantation Tutor of the Old Dominion*, edited by Hunter Dickinson Farish, Williamsburg, 1957, pp. 110, 195-196.

15. R. T. H. Halsey and Charles O. Cornelius, *A Handbook of the American Wing*, New York, 1924, pp. 111-112.

16. Léon Chotteau, *Les Français en Amérique*, Paris, 1876, quoted in Sherrill, *op. cit.* (footnote 8), p. 96.

17. Médéric Louis Elie Moreau de Saint-Méry, *Moreau de St. Méry's American Journey*, translated and edited by Kenneth Roberts and Anna M. Roberts, Garden City, 1947, p. 266.

18. Claude Blanchard, *The Journal of Claude Blanchard, Commissary of the French Auxiliary Army Sent to the United States During the American Revolution, 1780-1783*, translated by William Duane and edited by Thomas Balch, Albany, 1876, pp. 41, 49.

19. Moreau de Saint-Méry, *op. cit.* (footnote 17), p. 266.

20. François, Marquis de Barbé-Marbois, *Our Revolutionary Forefathers. The Letters of François, Marquis de Barbé-Marbois During His Residence in the United States as Secretary of the French Legation 1779-1785*, translated and edited by Eugene Parker Chase, New York, 1929, p. 123.

21. Nancy Shippen, *Nancy Shippen, Her Journal Book*, edited by Ethel Armes, Philadelphia, 1935, pp. 167, 229, 243.

22. Chastellux, *op. cit.* (footnote 9), quoted in Sherrill, *op. cit.* (footnote 8), p. 40.

23. Eliza Southgate Bowne, *A Girl's Life Eighty Years Ago. Selections from the Letters of Eliza Southgate Bowne*, edited by Clarence Cook, New York, 1887, p. 207.

24. Shippen, *op. cit.* (footnote 21), p. 167.

25. Prince de Broglie, "Journal du Voyage", *Mélanges de la Société des Bibliophiles Français*, Paris, 1903, quoted in Sherrill, *op. cit.* (footnote 8), p. 13.

26. Comte de Ségur, *Mémoires, ou Souveniresetet Anecdotes*, Paris, 1826, quoted in Sherrill, *op. cit.* (footnote 8), p. 78.

27. Shippen, *op. cit.* (footnote 21), p. 175.

28. Kalm, *op. cit.* (footnote 7), vol. 2, p. 677; Moreau de Saint-Méry, *op. cit.* (footnote 17), p. 286.

29. Shippen, *op. cit.* (footnote 21), p. 248.

30. François Jean, Marquis de Chastellux, *Travels in North America in the Years 1780-81-82*, New York, 1827, p. 114.

31. Ferdinand Marie Bayard, *Travels of a Frenchman in Maryland and Virginia, with a Description of Philadelphia and Baltimore in 1791*, translated and edited by Ben C. McCary, Ann Arbor, 1950, p. 48.

32. Mrs. Anne Grant, *Memoirs of an American Lady, with Sketches of Manners and Scenery in America, as They Existed Previous to the Revolution*, New York, 1846, p. 54.

33. Kalm, *op. cit.* (footnote 7), vol. 2, p. 611.

34. Barbé-Marbois, *op. cit.* (footnote 20), p. 123.

35. Blanchard, *op. cit.* (footnote 18), p. 78.

36. Ferdinand M. Bayard, *Voyage dans l'Intérieur des Etats-Unis*, Paris, 1797, quoted in Sherrill, *op. cit.* (footnote 8), p. 93.

37. Claude Victor Marie, Prince de Broglie, "Narrative of the Prince de Broglie", translated by E. W. Balch in *Magazine of American History*, April 1877, vol. I, p. 233.

38. Bayard, *op. cit.* (footnote 36), quoted in Sherrill, *op. cit.* (footnote 8), p. 93.

39. Brissot de Warville, *op. cit.* (footnote 6), p. 129.

40. Suffolk County [Massachusetts] Probate Court Record Books (hereinafter cited as Suffolk County Record Books), vol. 53, p. 444, inventory of Mrs. Hannah Pemberton, Boston, June 22, 1758; vol. 39, p. 185, inventory of Joseph Blake, Boston, September 18, 1746. Among other inventories in Suffolk County Record Books listing tea tables with tea equipment thereon were those of Sendal Williams, Boston, March 13, 1747 (vol. 43, p. 407); Revd. Dr. Benja. Colman, Boston, September 1, 1747 (vol. 40, p. 266); Mr. Nathl. Cunningham, February 6, 1748 (vol. 42, p. 156); Joseph Snelling, Boston, December 8, 1748 (vol. 42, p. 60); Eliza. Chaunay, Boston, May 28, 1757 (vol. 52, p. 382); Gillam Tailer, Boston, October 18, 1757 (vol. 52, p. 817); Jon. Skimmer, Boston, October 30, 1778 (vol. 77, p. 565).

41. Bayard, *op. cit.* (footnote 31), p. 47.

42. Letter from [Louis Guillaume] Otto [to Nancy Shippen], undated, Shippen Papers, box 6, Manuscripts Division, Library of Congress. The letter is dated about 1780 by Ethel Armes, *op. cit.* (footnote 21), p. 8.

43. Jacob Hiltzheimer, *Extracts from the Diary of Jacob Hiltzheimer of Philadelphia, 1765-1798*, edited by Jacob Cox Parsons, Philadelphia, 1893, p. 94.

44. Fithian, *op. cit.* (footnote 14), p. 193.

45. Benjamin Franklin, letter to Mrs. Deborah Franklin, dated February 19, 1758, London. *The Writings of Benjamin Franklin*, edited by Albert Henry Smyth, New York, 1905, vol. 3, p. 432.

46. Bayard, *op. cit.* (footnote 36), quoted in Sherrill, *op. cit.* (footnote 8), p. 93.

47. *Boston Gazette*, April 25, 1737; *Boston News-Letter*, June 24, 1762; *The New-York Gazette*, January 8, 1799. These and other newspaper references have been taken variously from the following sources: George Francis Dow, *The Arts and Crafts in New England, 1704-1775*, Topsfield, Massachusetts, 1927; Rita Susswein Gottesman, *The Arts and Crafts in New York, 1726-1776*, New York, 1938, and *The Arts and Crafts in New York, 1777-1799*, New York, 1954; and Alfred Coxe Prime, *The Arts and Crafts in Philadelphia, Maryland, and South Carolina, 1721-1785*, Topsfield, Massachusetts, 1929.

48. Suffolk County Record Books, vol. 39, p. 499, inventory of James Pemberton, Boston, April 8, 1747.

49. *Boston News-Letter*, November 28, 1771.

50. Shippen, *op. cit.* (footnote 21), p. 215.

51. *Boston News-Letter*, October 4, 1750; *Maryland Journal*, November 20, 1781.

52. Robin, *op. cit.* (footnote 1), p. 23.

53. W. Stephen Thomas, "Major Samuel Shaw and the Cincinnati Porcelain", *Antiques*, May 1935, vol. 27, p. 178. The letter and tea set are exhibited at Deerfield, Massachusetts, by the Heritage Foundation.

54. Fithian, *op. cit.* (footnote 14), p. 133.

55. Kalm, *op. cit.* (footnote 7), vol. 1, p. 191.

56. C. F. Volney, *Tableau du Climat et du Sol des Etats-Unis*, Paris, 1803, quoted in Sherrill, *op. cit.* (footnote 8), p. 95.

57. *Boston News-Letter*, March 24, 1774, November 18, 1742, and April 4, 1771; *New-York Journal*, August 3, 1775.

58. *New-York Gazette*, April 3, 1727; *Boston Gazette*, June 4, 1759; *Boston News-Letter*, January 9, 1772; *Maryland Gazette*, May 13, 1773; *Pennsylvania Journal*, December 15, 1763.

59. Kalm, *op. cit.* (footnote 7), vol. 1, p. 347.

60. *Boston News-Letter*, April 4, 1771, November 18, 1742, and January 9, 1772; *New-York Gazette*, February 14, 1757; *Pennsylvania Gazette*, January 25, 1759; *Rivington's New York Gazeteer*, January 13, 1774; *New-York Journal*, August 3, 1775; *Boston Gazette*, September 11, 1758; *New-York Daily Advertiser*, January 21, 1797.

61. Moreau de Saint-Méry, *op. cit.* (footnote 17), p. 38.

62. *New-York Gazette*, February 14, 1757; *Boston Gazette*, May 14, 1764; *Maryland Gazette*, January 4, 1759; *New-York Journal*, August 3, 1775; *Pennsylvania Gazette*, July 6, 1772, and October 31, 1781; *Boston News-Letter*, April 4, 1771, and January 9, 1772; *New-York Daily Advertiser*, January 21, 1797.

63. *New-York Mercury*, October 30, 1758; *Pennsylvania Journal*, April 25, 1765; *Boston News-Letter*, January 17, 1745; *New-York Gazette*, December 6, 1771.

64. *Pennsylvania Gazette*, January 25, 1759; *Pennsylvania Journal*, April 25, 1765; *Independent Journal* [New York], July 23, 1785.

65. *New-York Gazette*, April 3, 1727.

66. *Maryland Gazette*, January 4, 1759; *Pennsylvania Chronicle*, January 29, 1770; Suffolk County Record Books, vol. 52, p. 324, inventory of John Procter, May 13, 1757.

67. Suffolk County Record Books, vol. 52, p. 327, inventory of Revd. Charles Brockwell, May 13, 1757.

68. Quotations variously from *New-York Gazette*, April 3, 1727, August 2, 1762; *Commercial Advertiser* [New York], Oct. 10, 1797; *Boston Gazette*, July 26, 1756; *New-York Daily Advertiser*, May 7, 1793; *Boston News-Letter*, October 18, 1750; *Pennsylvania Evening Post*, July 11, 1776.

69. *New-York Journal*, August 3, 1775; *New-York Daily Advertiser*, January 21, 1797.

70. *Pennsylvania Packet*, May 29, 1775; *American Weekly Mercury* [Philadelphia], January 1736; *Boston Gazette*, May 3, 1751, and September 11, 1758; *Pennsylvania Journal*, August 1, 1771.

71. Bayard, *op. cit.* (footnote 36), quoted in Sherrill, *op. cit.* (footnote 8), p. 92.

72. *New-York Daily Advertiser*, May 7, 1793.

73. Letter from Otto Holland Williams to Dr. Philip Thomas, April 12, 1786, Williams Papers, vol. 4, letter no. 320. Manuscript, Maryland Historical Society, Baltimore, Maryland.

74. *Boston News-Letter*, April 4, 1771; *Pennsylvania Gazette*, October 31, 1781; *Minerva, & Mercantile Evening Advertiser* [New York], August 4, 1796.

75. *Boston News-Letter*, September 16, 1736.

Book Review

Please take a few moments to review on Amazon.

Jennifer loves to hear from her readers and to share stories and recipes.

Rather read the blog on your Kindle?

Blog: Over the Teacups http://www.overtheteacups.com

Facebook: Jennifer Petersen - Tea
https://www.facebook.com/JenniferPetersen.Tea/

Twitter – http://www.twitter.com/TeaMentor

Jennifer's Pinterest: http://www.pinterest.com/jpetersen01

To receive advance notice of future books by Jennifer Petersen, please visit our website
http://www.teatrademart.com.

Thank you very much for purchasing this book! I hope you enjoy it!

Printed in Great Britain
by Amazon